THOUGHT BY CHANCE

GREAT THOUGHTS JUST STRIKES BY CHANCE

MANYA JOHARI

Copyright © Manya Johari
All Rights Reserved.

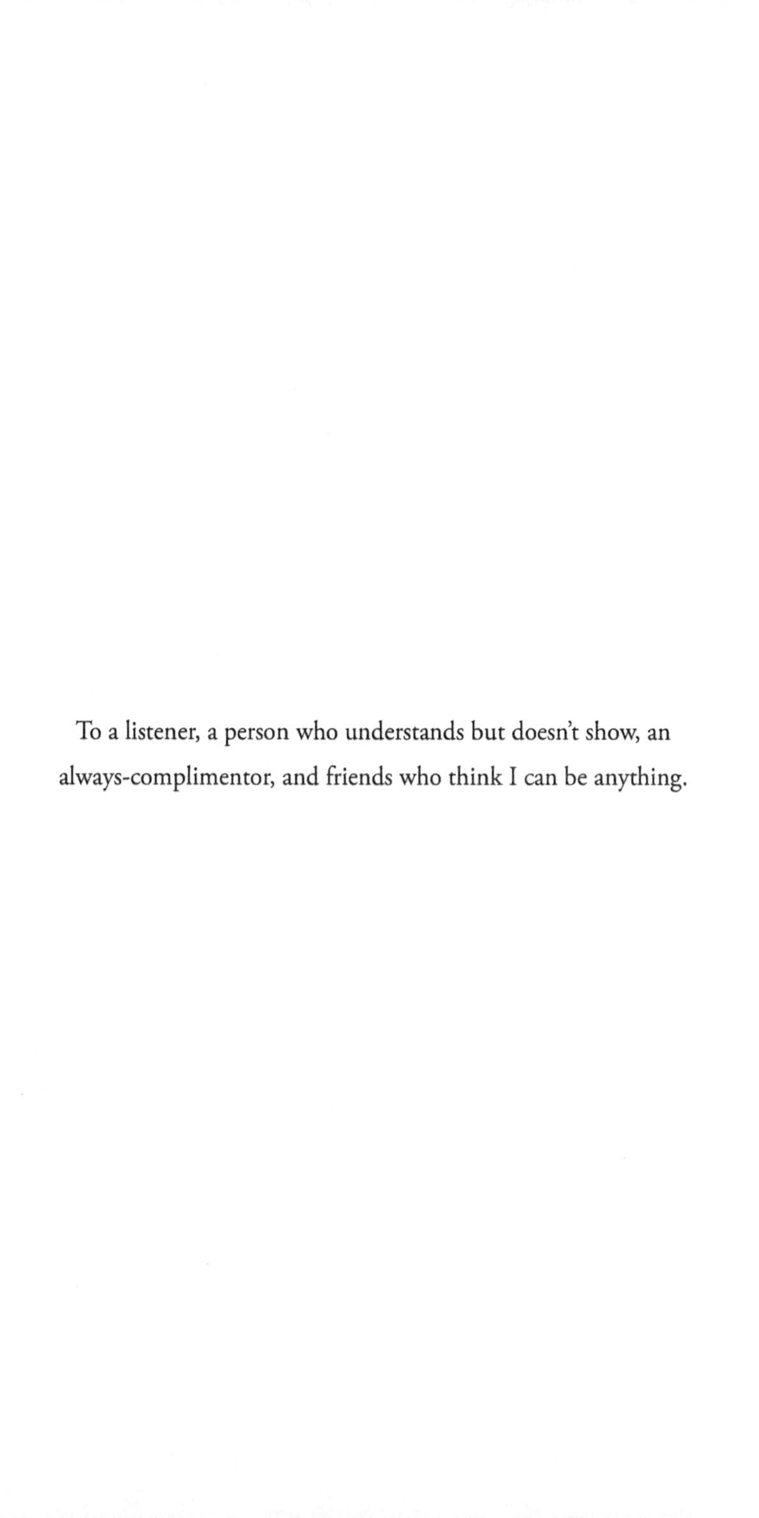

To a listener, a person who understands but doesn't show, an always-complimentor, and friends who think I can be anything.

Contents

Contents

Preface

there was a girl who was just 5.

    didn't had too much to do,

    so she picked up a pen and paper,

    and started to write whatever she sees and feels.

    slowly the written pieces came together and formed her first poem.

    she loved the way her words started leaving a deep meaning,

    this lead her to all new world of expression.

    where she wrote all that she feels,

    and at the end, she was able to make a collection of all the little thoughts in her head.

    so, now the thing in your hand is not a book but thoughts of that little head.

1. An Inspiration

Inspiration to change the world,
Inspiration to tell the world,
that there is someone,
somewhere,in a lane orAn Inspiration
area that is plain.

Inspiration is all around just open your eyes,
what you are looking for is just beside your sight.
Inspiration can make you alimb up the mount,
or take you deep in the ocean's snout.
Just tighten your belts to explor the world,
and observe yourself to be inspired by the world.

2. I am going

Those things that had perfect place are now homeless.
Places that had the particular name are now nameless.
Faces that were clear are getting blur
Guidelines that were guiding are now not audible
People that were caring are now not here.

alone as a fighter fish
unknown as a stranger
trapped as a caged bird
illiterate as a child
I am going

3. Quotation

"Till you are alive be happy and enjoy it but if you are dieing then double enjoy it so that the people would remember you as the person of smile and who laughed till his last breath."

4. Think of a world

Think of a world where there is no rule of human brain,
but of free spirits.
Think of a world where eyes were not closed for dark,
but to dream high.
Think of a world where no heart is crushed or pushed,
but where it pumps high to reach high.
Think of a world where are not cuffed or stopped,
but allowed to do something new.

How do you think this world can be made?
Nothing more than just some love and care,
for all those who are weak,
all those who can't dream,
all those who can't pump their heart free,
all those who are not allowed to do something new.
This love and care will just bring a new world that you have
never thought of.

5. Remember them

Remember the waves that gave you thought to sail,
who pussed you to across the mighty sea.
The waves were your roots of achievement,
and the success gained.

Remember the storms that made you strong,
who pulled you out to say "stand again and play."
The storms were your stems of determination,
and the willpower you made.

Remember the day when your father said,
"that's my child with name and fame."
His words were your fruit of hard work,
and the struggle you faced.

6. Quotation

"*Till then you cannot live your life, you can't make anyone else to live it.* "

7. Behind

See human what have you done,
footsteps of yours had become signs of destruction,
your hands of creativity are old causing earth cold.

Mind of your wisdom is now a whole distraction.
The words of sense are now causing voilence.
See human what have you done.

My dear human,
sand is still there,
so, wake up and don't let it go

8. hunting myself

Time pass about had gone,
Time going on will pass,
Time going to come will end.

Take chair at the side, with the corner of your wit,
it might tell you to get up,
but tell it not to peep.

Set yourself away as far as you can be,
from this mighty world,
toward yourself that is in a deep dark heart-core cave.

See what you had found, it's you in a different form,
lets us see what you can be,
that's not the question, as you can be anything.

Wake up now and hunt yourself in the passing time,
now answer me who are you,
are you the one you found or the one that we made?
....

9. Quotation

"If you have been broken in seven parts then get ready to be broken down again in ten because life is all breaking and self build."

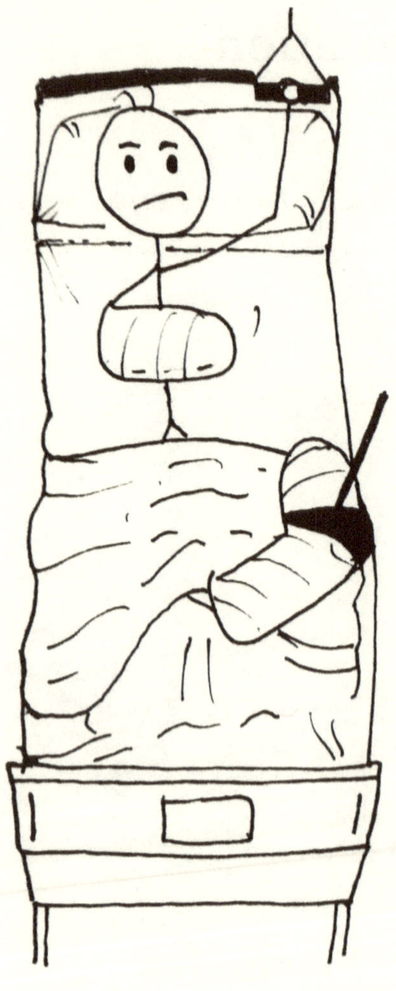

10. The corpse

A corpse buried deep in me,
and the graveyard would be named hear.t
The corpse belongs to me,
as I murdered it.

I keep it down, depressed,
in pressure that even I couldn't bear,
as long as it survived,
it gave voice to all my sin.

Since it died I do not realize,
the thing I am doing was going worst.
The corpse still tries to become immortal,
but I don't think it could survive.

As long the corpse is in me,
I regret his life and go back to ease.
but that corpse is still,
yelling with all his mighty will.

He hopes that I could hear,
the will of its goes in favor.
I don't want to ignore,

but I thought to have no other way.

The corpse is still buried but,
tries to be alive.
I dugged it out and asked,
to forgive me for your end.

11. Aim

• 13 •

aim for time
not for the clock
aim for height
not for the mount
aime for shine
not for the sun
aim for worth
not for the price

aim you have is hard but great
is easy for them who see it as a play
aim i have is thoughts of gay
but it is daydream say the bay

12. Quotation

• 14 •

"*God had made this world and Imagination had developed it.*"

13. Who can divide me?

Who can divide me in religion?
As I salute in the mosque and where the Hindus pray,
I bow my head in front of him so as to the Christ,
Then who is the one to divide me?
raised the question who am I?

Who can divide me in the caste?
As I teach in the temple and rule as the king,
I trade as a merchant and work so as to make the world clean,
Then who is the one to divide me?
Raised the question who am I

Who can divide me into gender?
As I manage the home and the office,
I work as a man do so as the work, I should do,
Then who is the one to divide me?
Raised the question who am I?

14. Running against

We are running,
Against the wind,
Towards the shined,
To be finned.

We are running,
Against the odds,
Towards the god,
To be called.

We are running,
Against the kind,
Towards the mind,
To find.

15. Quotation

"Life is something that is like time, Once it passed away the life moments missed woud not come back."

16. A Unique You

• 19 •

My dear heart tear,

mind of glow,

and the soul you own,

mixed up and create you,

for me, my thoughts of clear.

love for you will never end,

till I am here and you are there.

You my dear lovely hare,

with mouth of ear.

17. Use

What mean to have a sun that does not rise?
What mean to have a day that does not work?
What mean to have a car that no one drives?
What mean to have a house where no one lives?

Things are useful till then used.
The body is useful till it is been moved.
Watch is useful till it shows the time.
And our brain is useful till we make it work.

18. Quotation

"Difficult ways lead to Learning."

19. Bothways

I just got up,
from the nap I took,
and the vision I looked,

I am the one who saw,
the multiple forms of me,
that resides in me;

I am the one who walked
on both roads of life,
from the diversion added in my way;

I am the one who experienced
the pain, sorrow, and happiness in vain,
Hence, could not fathom the beauty of this game;

I am the one who leaped
from the steepest cliff and
the one who was buried in endless grief;

I am the one who killed,
a soul of my own,

by the pressure that I cant hold;

And the one who brings it back to life to survive more,
The coin had two faces before
but I had lived its every phase that still cant be seen.

20. I am

I am the soul-deep within.
I am the heart to love within.
I am the breath that you take within.
I am the one who tests you.
I am the one who trusts you.
I am the one who loves you.
And the one who leaves you.

Who am I?
I am your life living within.

21. Quotation

"Problems are there is everyone life some move on it and some move with it."

22. Life

Life is what you care,
with a share.
Life is what you spend,
with a bend.
Life is what you talk,
with a walk.
Life is what you read,
with someone indeed.

Life is like a river in the air,
and mount on your bed.
Butterfly in your stomach,
and a world of headaches.
life is a most unbelievable fact,
that cannot be found in science,
or in anyone's mind.

23. Other world

Now I like the other world,
as it is pleasantly set.
Life of people is much like a play,
that makes me out in gay.

Now I like the other world,
because life looks pretty cool there,
problems come and vanish in seconds,
no need to cry in pain.

Now I like the other world,
cause' people in there have a comical sense,
which makes them happy on a badest day.
I like the way they make me laugh by laughing at themselves.

Now I like the other world,
as the endings are always happy ones.
not to guess, not to say,
The end is always simple as fine molded clay.

24. Quotation

25. Living

Living on earth is so unique.
Once it falls and,
the next it rises.

Once it showers and,
the next, it drys.

We wonder looking up what is next,
but the answer always remains the same.
Living on earth is so unique.

Once there will be dark and,
the next, it turns into light.

Our life has moods and emotions,
knotted together with every ner string,
that's why it is said living on earth is so unique.

26. Scared of

I'm scared of shadows that follow me.
I'm scared of this world that pushes me.
I'm scared of the dark that makes me lost.

But shadows follow to give confidence,
And world teaches us not to give up,
Dark indicates that there will be a time to come out and shine
bright.

27. Quotation

"*Life is once and all don't waste it on those who can destruct it in a second.*"

28. I wonder

I wonder why I am here,
I wonder why I am made,
I wonder what I have to do ,
what he had written for me.

Something different or,
something common.
Something big or,
something small.

Targets are big and wishes are huge, dreams are unlimited, and achievements are few.
What to do, or what not to do, the question is difficult enough.
Life is short, time is limited, how to use, and how to spend,
what can be done for great or for wellbeing.

Eyes are filled and mouth is murmuring,
at last, the mind is confused and also empty
what to fill cannot be thought of.
It is difficult to live in.

29. Can you sense it?

Can feel the lifefulness,
of these lifeless words?

Can you see the beauty,
of this woody dark world?

Can you smell the aroma,
of the scentless ends?

Can you hear the sound,
of this silent cold?

Can you taste the experience,
of these dancing souls?

Can you touch the emotions,
of these emotionless ink?

30. Quotation

"Sadness is like morning dew that comes everyday in the morning, but disappears when sunlight enters, a warmth of support and light of love spreads in and starts your day."

31. Clock of life

A bunch of clocks hovering over me,
reminding the left,
and forcing the best,
to happen with me.

I closed my eyes,
so that I can't see,
doing the wrongest deed,
after a while clock stopped,

and I started peeping,
between my fingers and I thought,
now I am free,
but got a thought that, key

opened a thing that the,
clocks doesn't stopped but it's me.
I set the clocks with the whole eye opened
and started the doings again.

32. Left alone

Alone in the mid-way flow,
finding someone who can row,
every time I am left behind with the same question that,
why didn't anyone come?

I stayed alone in mid-way flow,
when started myself to row,
no one was ever there for me,
but I was always there as a beam.

Never let anyone down,
but everyone left me to frown.
The tears I dropped were never counted.
The hurdles I faced had never stopped.

Tears had a count,
and hurdles had stopped,
cause' now i have a partner
who is me, myself.

33. Quotation

34. A golden bird

There was a bird that used to fly so high,
got a fear of heights.
This fear was planted in her,
as others get burns from her golden wings.

She slowly forgot to even fly,
and started crumbling on the land.
Her feathers started losing their shine,
this is what she thought of herself.

Once rolling down a row,
she heard someone saying,
that her fly was awesome but,
some burnt planted a fear seed in her.

The bird got a shock in her head climbed up a tree and flapped
her wings,
The shine of her wings was replenished as there was some dust
covering it,
got the words, and flew the highest,
the bird was now like a star in the daylight.

35. Thought

Brain I have,
is filled with threads,
of different odds.
Is a storehouse of bulbs,
holding up my day bright.
Is a graveyard of pics,
that had taken me down.
And is home for words,
healing blisters, and giving wounds.

My brain can lead me to mountains of clouds,
and drown me to last earth's bed.
Life works on a simple principle,
grow and let grow,
learn and let learn,
breath and let breath.

36. Quotation

"*Sometimes, something really bad happens to warn us for the worst outcomes of our deeds.*"

37. Spotlight

Light should be redeemed by my personality,
my smile should bring glitter to the day,
and my nature must define "the beauty".
I am a spotlight but by my inner self.

My habit should attract,
my core should protect,
and my way should appreciate.
I am a spotlight but by my inner self.

This is not just attention, it's me,
this is not to please, it's me,
and neither of this is the trend, it's me.
I am a spotlight but by my inner self.

38. My dream

I started weaving a beautiful dream,
and when it was at its peak.
I woke up and ran towards it,
and was determined to fulfill it.

As I was going to start my way,
I stopped at a heavy beam,
crossing it needed my weapons,
but they were already diminished by big heads,

I cried not to do that,
but my head was crushed at the bottom,
then a ray of light fell over me,
and asked me to follow it,

it told me to build my own weapons,
which could not easily be broken,
putting day and night on my hand,
I made it, too powerful to break that beam.

Now I am free.
I am powerful and never weak.
Just got some knowledge that guided me,

and led me to fulfill my dreams.

39. Quotation

"A line has the power to hold you back and if you go beyond, learn how to fight."

40. Our love ones

The day I reached the earth you were there.
The time I opened my eyes you were there.
The place I started mumbling you were there.
The thing I picked up first you were there.
The floor I walked upon first you were there.

My whole life I would love to have you both here till I have
completed my work here.
You are breath I breathe.
You are the word I speak.
You are my heart that beats,
And mind that is always grateful to God to give you both to
me.

41. All about a heart

I met a beautiful heart,
who feels what he sees,
and see what he feels.

He was a sensitive one,
but he can't be called weak,
because he was as strong as a mighty ship.

He falls then stands,
and stands then falls,
but he loves this process as it goes on.

I whispered to him,
why are you like this?
he just smiled and said,

This is what you wanted to be,
I am just a medium to seek,
a beautiful land of your dream.

42. Quotation

"Disability does not mean, your disabled part but your disabled mind is the mastermind behind your pain and sorrow they are nothing but the illusions created by your own mind. "

43. Diversion

A girl with high dream,
got up to a diversion,
road of her dreams has made many bends,
want to choose it,

but was pushed to the other one,
I heard her saying this road is better,
I couldn't tell her,
that wasn't her way.

She jumped in joy and played with gay,
and there come a board,
signed "***dead end***"
she ignored it and carried on,

but the way became worst,
every step gave her pain,
and sorrow that made her out in vain,
she yelled and cried for a diverse,

that would lead her back,
to the way she left back,
she tried all her will out,

at last, she found a painful way,

But after she follows it,
all the obstacles were not so hard,
as she has gone through the worst,
now her wounds have healed and she is back to joy again.

44. Rush

Rush is the basic necessity of human life.
A house along a lane,
allows the mediums to pass by.
Lives up a humble lady watching the passing time.
Sun comes up, she rase a smile,
and seeoff him when he goes to rest.

Her life is all of peace,
that is the thing she loves the most.
In the house hangs up a balcony,
with a curve approaching out,
and is always occupied with plants,
that remain as green as she is.

Rush of thoughts she observe from above,
differs a lot is her mind, but
shares a common point how to live and survive.
Rushing orchestra of horns make her think,
do this would really cause any change,
to the people in other world and
that who have no aims.

She shares her thoughts through her eyes,

and let herself enjoy her peaceful life.
The sun sets down and the moon is high,
she still stands at the balcony for sight,
her time goes around and her heart fills up,
when she realises the rush of life.

She goes back to bed and closes her eyes,
with the thoughts and learnings,
she received by the daysight.

45. Quotation

"Pain is pain, you can't reset it; it's just how much you wanna feel it."

Art needs a medium but feeling does not.